MARTIAL MAXIMS
A Codex of Martial Strategies

武戰略諺語法典

By TYLER REA

DISCLAIMER WARNING!

This book contains self defense strategies that can cause Physical injury. The author assume no responsibility For any injury, misuse or damage resulting from the applications of the self defense strategies presented here.   Always train with safety under the Guidance of a Qualified instructor. Consult your physician before Using this or any exercise program.

This Codex is a collection of Martial art stratagems, tactics, wisdom & principles of Ancient Martial training. It is of utmost importance not to simply collect knowledge but to perceive deeper endless layers of meaning nested in knowledge.

一條心，一個身體，一個電源
- One Mind, One Body, One Power.

如果你追逐兩隻兔子，你會抓不住
專注於一個攻擊的時間
- If you chase after two rabbits, you'll catch neither. Focus on one attacker at a time.

那些未能獲得一個以上的
逃離活該死
- Those who fail to secure more than one Escape invite Death.

一個聰明的動物有三窟
一個聰明的武術備份有三種形式
或三種形式逸出
- A clever Animal has three burrows.
A clever Martial artist has three forms of Back-up or three forms of escape.

如果你不殺根雜草會回來
- If you don't kill the Root the weed will return.
  (Destroy the attackers structural support.)

覆巢之下當所有的雞蛋都碎了，
當攻擊者所有潛在的平衡被
打破攻擊被推翻

- When a Nest is overturned all eggs are broken,
When the Attackers balance is broken all potential
attacks are overturned.

嘗試任何在絕望的情況下。
- Try anything in a desperate situation.

兩起襲擊事件是一體的，沒有一個攻擊
對於成功的概率最高
引人注目的部署多個攻擊

- Two Attacks are one, and one attack is none.
For the highest probability of successful
striking deploy multiple attacks.

尋求主宰直接從頂部的外橋接觸參考
- Seek to dominate straight from the outside
top bridge contact reference.

尋求旋轉與滾動力由內而
外底橋接觸參考
- Seek to Turn & roll force from the inside bottom
bridge contact reference.

在第一次接觸中，攻擊者必
須屬於自己的馬

- At first contact the attacker must fall of their horse.
(Break the vertical structure support of the spine.)

隱藏刺敵人找到

- Hide thorns for the enemy to find.

沉肘，奪回控制權

- Sink the Elbow to regain control.

使用剪切力引導攻擊
使用鑽探力驅動的攻擊者

- Use Shearing force to steer the attacker.
Use Drilling force to drive the attacker.

緊緊地擠在腋下

- *Chong Jao* (Tightly squeeze close the armpits.)

手不要退縮向前延伸

- *Lurn Sao Bot Gwai Choi Sao Juen -*
(The hands don't draw back to extend forward.)

拉的胸部，推出上背部，
並帶來尾骨

- Pull in the chest, push out the upper back,
and bring in the tail bone.

可以形成一個金字塔的重心在中心
- Form a pyramid with the center of gravity in the center.

肘部，肩膀，腰部下沉
- Sink the elbows, the shoulders, and the waist.

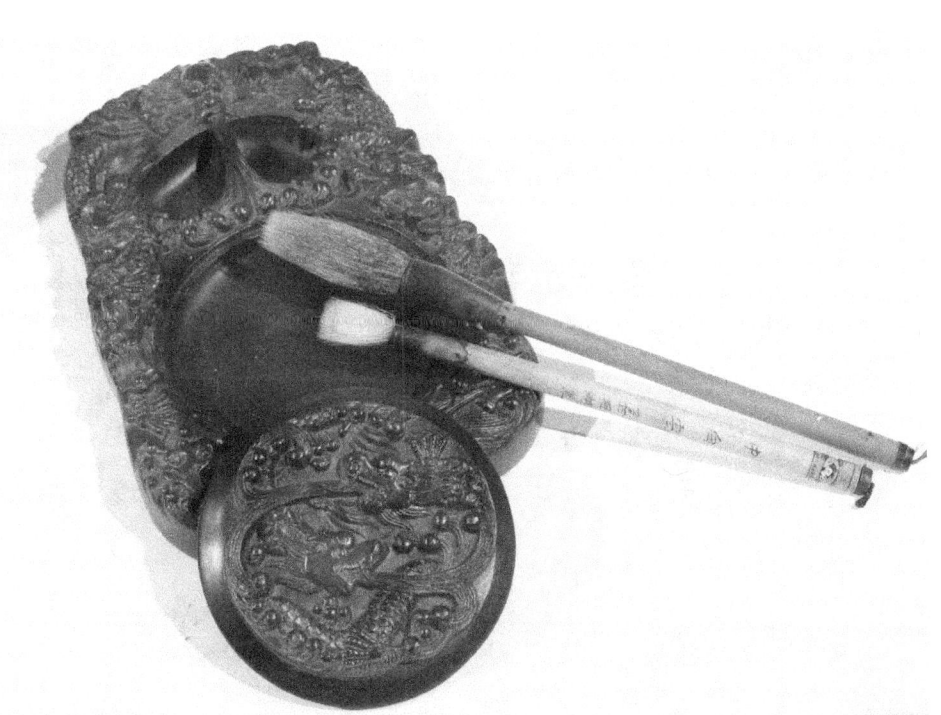

残逼切截展

Hate your enemy so much, you grind your
teeth and want to beat him .

追随抖摔连

to chase and follow, to shake and throw
and make the attacks continuously

冷弹脆快硬

The power should be precise,
springy, crispy, fast and hard.

神意气力闲

The spirit, the mind, and strength should
all be focused and calm.

急流勇似电

Powerful & direct like lighting ,rapidly flowing forward
(to crush anything in the way)

对敌似婴玩

To face an enemy, like a Cat attacking a mouse

胆大心要细

To have a brave heart with a cautious intellect.

含情致胜难

Victory is elusive, if you have mercy in your heart.

言甘意中恶

Speak with Tact, act with focused intent.

手毒是真传

Fighting with heavy hands (without mercy)
is the real combat focus.

临敌心莫惧

Your heart shouldn't be in fear
when you fight your enemy.

动机在眼前

Seek an opportunity to make a move.

远不贪不即

if your opponent is too far,
don't be greedy to press ahead.

近不离不欠

if the opponent is close by, don't let
him get away to create distance.

出手招要快

When extending the hands out to attack ,
the combinations MUST be be fast!

气胜意占先

Your fighting spirit should be greater, and your
mind should be 9 steps ahead of the attackers.

不犯招架打

Don't fight according to his rhythm or plan, Fight using your skills to defeat the opponent.

有触手要连

As soon as hand contact is made,
Attack should deploy one after another.

动中意常静

The mind should be calmly
focused during the movements.

静里动在先

When in stillness, the mind is advancing ahead.

动静随机变

Advance or stop according to the opportunity,
never retreat or retract unless it's unavoidable

虚实有何难

Transitions between fake and real (hollow and solid)
movements should be easy.

操时情中有

When training, always imagine a real fight, using genuine
applications devoid of wasted movement.

用时形内含

When applied it in fight , Power will always
originate from correct, rooted structure.

得艺必试敌
Test your knowledge, focus on practicality.

真假易显然
Your Martial knowledge whether correct/accurate
or not can be easily judged.

神形归妙处
When training body and spirit all
advance to a high level.

功夫是蒂荃
To cultivate Martial Gong Fu
virtue is the main focus.

Essentials of Boxing Structure

头要顶 — The Head needs to be pulled up.

项要竖 — The neck needs to stand up.

目要睹 — The eyes need to be fixed on the opponent.

口要闭 — The mouth needs to be closed .

舌要抵 —The tongue needs to be pressed up against the palate

齿要扣 — The teeth need to bite together.

肩要沉 — The shoulders need to sink & root down.

肘要坠 — The elbows need to be lowered & root down.

臂要夹 — The arms need to move against each other in polorized differential rotation. (like that of Yin & Yang) to express a rope twisting kind of energy, Ging).

腰要拧 — The waist needs to be turned or twisted through rooted rotation.

手要对 — The hands need to be aliened to each other, each Guarding the it's side of the center line plane corridor.

指要撑 — The fingers need to be straight and expand forward.

身要揉 — The body should manifest a unified Toroidal, vorticular power in all vector planes.

胸要虚 — The chest needs to be hollowed.

胯要裹 — The hips need to be wrapped down, tailbone rolled forward.

肛要兜 — Tighten up the Kegel muscles to strengthen the pelvic floor "grain path"

膝要提 — Knees need to be raised to be agile.

足要蹬 — Feet need to Deng(push from the heel).

趾要抓 — Toes need to grab the ground after step down.

MARTIAL MAXIMS

Sau Gay Loot Soong Syeung Moh Duck
Remain disciplined—conduct yourself ethically
as a martial artist.

Ming Lai Yee Ngoy Goke Juen Chun
Practice courtesy and righteousness—serve the community and
respect your elders.

Ngoy Toang Hock Tuen Geet Loke Kwun
Love your fellow students—be united and avoid conflicts.

Jeet Sick Yoke Boh Sau Jing Sun
Limit your desires and pursuit of bodily pleasures—preserve the
proper spirit.

Kun Leen Jop Gay But Lay Sun
Train diligently—maintain your skills.

Hock Yeung Hay Gai Lum Dau Jung
Learn to develop spiritual tranquility—abstain from arguments
and fights.

Syeung Chue Sai Tai Doh Wun Mun
Participate in society—be conservative and gentle in your manners.

Foo Yeuk Siu Yee Moh Foo Yun
Help the weak and the very young—use your martial skills for
the good of humanity.

Gai Gwong Soy Hoan Gay Joh Fun
Pass on the tradition—preserve this Chinese art and its Rules of
Conduct.

Gau Foong Yiu Han
You must be ferocious when clashing

Chuet Kuen Yiu Fai — The fist must be fast

Fot Lick Yiu Ging
Power must be used to release strength

See Gan Yiu Joon
Timing must be accurate

Fon Sau Yiu Leen
Trapping Hands must be continuous

Hay Lick Yiu Lau
Some of your strength must be kept in reserve

Ying Sai Yiu Sau
Your own posture must be protected

Ngon Sun Yiu Gau
Eye power and focus must be sharp

Yiu Ma Yiu Hup
The waist and stance must be united

Sau Gyeuk Yiu Ying
Hands and feet must be coordinated

Doang Joke Yiu Ling
Movements must be agile

Yum Yeung Yiu Sick
The principles of Yin and Yang must be comprehended

Sum Jing Yiu Ging
The spirit must remain calm

Hay Lick Yiu Ding
Breathing and strength must be steady

Loy Hay Yiu Chum
Internal strength must be sunken

Moh Sai Yiu Wai
The fighting demeanor must be commanding

Kuet Jeen Yiu Jook
A fight must end quickly

Tai Yeuk Lick Seen Sau Wai Jop But Hoh Lau
A weak body must start Do not keep any bad habits with strength improvement

• Masters are made not born.

• The shifting of a single pillar will shake all the beams, Attack the root of structure

• Best to bestow a single skill on a student than a thousand pieces of gold.

• Posses a single skill, and reap the benefits for a lifetime.

• Maintain your focus and you can bore through an army of ten thousand opponents.

• Boldness of execution stems from superb skill.

• In the area of learning, age makes no
Difference, those who know will always be the teacher of others.

- Study and Inquiry are the path to knowledge.

- One Mind, One Body, One Power.

- Strike first and prevail, Strike late and fail.

- In Drama skill depends on the Lips, in Martial arts skill depends on the footwork.

- There is always one thing to subdue another, everything can be countered.

- Forced memorization is not as good as natural realization, this is an organic Martial awakening.

- Unity is Strength, - Structural Unity can turn dirt into Gold.

- If you chase after two rabbits, you'll catch neither. Focus on one attacker at a time.
- Those who fail to secure more than one
Escape deserve to die.

- A clever Animal has three burrows, A clever Martial artist has three forms of Back-up or three forms of escape.

- Heaven will reward the Diligent.

- When the time comes to apply knowledge, we always regret our lack thereof.

- A good quality of another may provide the remedy or solution for our own faults.

- You can't gain knowledge without practice, Wisdom comes from experience. Fall behind in practice and your skills will fade.

- Sand is minute, but it will harm your Eyes.
(Any attack is an Attack.)

• Those who bully the weak are cowards before the strong.

• If you strike someone with your fists,
Beware of a kick in return.

• Diligence is a priceless treasure, and Caution is a talisman for survival.

• If you don't kill the Root the weed will return.

• When a Nest is overturned all eggs are broken, When the Attackers balance is broken all potential attacks are overturned.

• Try anything in a desperate situation.

• Two Attacks are one, and one attack is none. For the highest probability of successful
striking deploy multiple attacks.

• Emphasize power, speed, accuracy,
Balance, aggressiveness.

• The techniques are quickly chained.

• Seek to dominate straight from the outside top bridge contact reference.

• Seek to Turn & roll force from the inside bottom bridge contact reference.

• At first contact the attacker must fall of their horse
(Off balance).

• The first Strike must make the attacker taste their spine.
(Break the vertical structure support of the spine).

• Attack until the Fist is soaked Red. *(Until it appears covered with a crimson glove.)*

• Hide thorns for the enemy to find.

• Sink the Elbow to regain control.

• Use Shearing force to steer the attacker.

• Use Drilling force to drive the attacker.

• The four Aims are: Shocking power, Sticky hands, releasing hands and heavy power.

• *Hum Hon* (Collapse & Swallow the chest).

• *Bat Boi* (Hunch back).

• *Chong Jao* (Tightly squeeze close the armpits).

• *An Dao Sao Dao* (The eyes and hands act together).

• *Yao Kiu Kiu Cern Gor -*
(If there is a bridge, then cross it.)

• *Mo Kiu Kiu Ha Cheun -*
(If there is no bridge, then make one.)

• *Yao Kiu Kiu Soi Kiu -*
(If there is a bridge, then Break it.)

• *Yao Kiu Kiu Gop Kiu -*
(If there is a bridge, then Trap it.)

• *Lurn Sao Bot Gwai Choi Sao Juen -*
(The hands don't draw back to extend forward.)

• Each movement must be packed into your Bone Marrow.

- Practice once a day, & you gain a Day. Skip a Day and you will loose ten days.

- Strive to remain calm in the midst of motion; loosen up the muscles and relax the mind.

- When entering, dominate the outside top Bridge reference, to control the situation.

- Do not collide with a strong opponent; with a weak opponent use a direct frontal assault.

- A quick fight should be ended quickly; no delay can be allowed.

- Use the three joints of the arm to prevent entry by the opponent's bridge; jam the opponent's bridge to restrict his movement.

- Iron fingers can strike a vital point at once.

- The stepping in elbow strike has sufficient threatening power.

- The phoenix eye punch has no equal.

- Springy power and the extended arm are applied to close range.

- Power starts from the heart and shoots towards the centerline.

- Power can be released in the intended manner; use of the line and position will be proper and hard to defeat.

- There is no difference in who started to study first; the one who achieves accomplishment is first.

- When facing multiple opponents, it is easy to manage the situation.

- When pushing the opponent's elbow, beware of being pulled.

• Learning the techniques without developing the skills will never bring any accomplishment.

• The ideal in Martial Arts is humanitarianism. Accomplishment uses diligence as a goal.

• When Wrist touch Wrist, A kick does not miss.

• Power is generated from the joints. Strength originates from the heels.

• Know the difference between Yin and Yang, real and feigned. Take advantage of any available opportunity.

• Beware of brute strength when facing someone from the same style.

• Principle of **Triple A (AAA)** - *Accept - Adapt - Act*

• In uniting the waist with the stance, power can be generated and directed anywhere.

• In a match do not expect any compassion.

• Grasping the throat is a ruthless technique. Once commenced, it cannot be stopped.

• Storing energy resembles pulling a bow. Releasing power is like shooting an arrow.

• Circular and straight accompany each other. Bent and straight complement one another.

• Extreme softness enables one to be hard. Being extremely natural enables one to be agile.

• Use alterations in stepping forward and backward. Hands and feet should be closely coordinated.

• As long as you are sticking to your opponent, you are unlikely to lose. A well trained waist can prevent loss of balance.

• Hand techniques must follow the Yin Yang principle. Strength must be applied with inner power. There is a counteraction to every attack.

• Rapid moves are hard to guard against. Go in when the opponent slows down.

• The feet are like wheels, and the hands like arrows.

• A hand used for attack serves also to parry.

• Do not collide with a strong arm bridge. Get out of the way and take initiative to attack.

• Each formula has a two or more person breakdown.

• White Eyebrow fighting is relaxed, continuous and flowing. The techniques are practiced exactly the way they are used;

There is no show.

• Principle of **3D's** - *Deflect - Displace - Destroy*
(Control at first contact.)

• Avoid flying elbow disease (Fei Jang), Drop your elbows, relax & sink your shoulders. (Jang Dai Lik) Elbow sinking power makes all of Heaven submit.

• Greet the Attacker with pain, Chase the Attacker with death.

• Go forward, Penetrate and displace.

- Beware of sneak attacks, leakage attacks, and Invisible center line attacks.

- Soft and relaxed strength will put your Opponent in jeopardy.

- Coordinate the hands and feet. Movement is integrated & unified.

- The Yin Yang power arc principle should be thoroughly understood.

- Upon achieving the highest level of proficiency, the application of techniques will vary according to the opponent.

- Simultaneous offense and defense, use offense as defense - Lin sil dai dar -- A hand used for attack serves also to parry.

- Move first to gain initiative, Attack according to timing

- Do not be too eager to strike, Do not be afraid to strike.

- Persistent attack will surely gain you entry. Staying on the defensive too long will surely get you into trouble.

- Cultivate & maintain a rooted pivot axis.
- Unite the three Kinetic springs of the Body - (Legs, Spine, Arms)

- Maintain a strong Triangular displacement bridge - (Som kwok kiu)

- Defend the 4 Gates - (Say Moon.)

- Kicking to the head is like punching to the foot. Kicks lose nine times out of ten.

- Simultaneous offense and defense, use offense as defense - Lin sil dai dar,
- A hand used for attack serves also to parry.

• The stance and steps are like a chariot, the hands are a on-slaught of arrows.

• Never force an opening. It must be developed & found through superior sticking & cultivated skill. When the opportunity is there, Your hands find it through sensitive feeling and touch.

• During sticky hand practice, the hand which has entered beyond the elbow will win nine times out of ten.

• Do not follow, force, or butt against the opponent's hands.

• Destroying the opponent's center line will control his bridge.

• A raised elbow weakens the force.

• The elbow root must be strong, Then you can take on any attack.

• If the opponent grasps your arm bridge, do not oppose him with brute force. Go with the opponent's force and apply your Turning skills to control the situation.

• The Say Ging "4 Energies" of Float, Sink, Swallow and Spit are the root of all skills.

• Go forward, Executing three attacks together.

• Soft and relaxed strength will put your Opponent in jeopardy.

• Coordinate the hands and feet. Movement is integrated & unified.

• Upon achieving the highest level of proficiency, the application of techniques will vary according to the opponent.

- Techniques come from the center

- Move first to gain initiative, Attack according to timing

- Persistent attack will surely gain you entry. Staying on the defensive too long will surely get you into trouble.

- Hold the head and neck straight, keep the tailbone tucked under, stay alert.

- Flowery techniques (Moi Fa) should not be used in sticky hand practice.

- Students from the same teacher will differ In their skills.

- Sink the elbows, shoulders, & the waist.

- Touching opponent's arm bridge makes the
    Situation more favorable.

- When pushing opponent's elbow, beware
    Of being pulled.

- Drop Elbows to take the center.

- Hands match hands, Kicks match kicks.

- Jam opponent's bridge. ***Bik Ging***

- Create a bridge if opponent's bridge is not present.

- The posture complements the hands to eject the opponent.

- The thrusting and fast attacks are well suited for closing in.

- Pull in the chest, push out the upper back, and bring in the tail bone.

- Form a pyramid with the center of gravity in the center.

- Sink the elbows, the shoulders, and the waist.

- Hold the head and neck straight and keep the spirit alert.

- Eyes are level, looking straight ahead, and watching all directions.

- Develop a good foundation for advanced techniques.

- Do not keep any bad habit.

(Sei Ging) 4 Kinds Of Ging Power Expression

崩擁塞 — *Beng Bik*
(Deep crashing,
Penetrating jamming)

炸 — *Zha*
(exploding)

驚彈 — *Jing tan*
(shocking, springy)

抖擻 — *Dou sou*
(Jolting shudder; Sudden shaking,
like a dog shaking the water off)

當步進，提高膝蓋彷彿被吸進民進

- When stepping, raise the knee as if it is being sucked into the Dan tien.

當移動手臂，根肘，如果它被吸進胸骨

- When moving the arm, root the elbow as if it is being sucked into the sternum.

當移動臂，廢的排骨用肘部

- When moving the arm, scrap the ribs with the elbow.

當進入一扇門，知道的鉸鏈，
門把手和中央開口

- When entering a door, know the hinges, door knobs and central opening.

- Martial interpretation -

Always be aware of the mid centerline both on a vertical and horizontal plane.

始終注意中期中心線垂直和水平平面上
鉛膝蓋必須永遠不會退去，
搖晃或固定探測器

- The lead knee must NEVER recede, wobble or be unanchored.

在所有的腰部旋轉，像一塊濕毛巾，
撐主角腿大腿，表達一個漩渦旋轉，
螺旋向上或向下移動。膝蓋絕不能退卻！

• In all waist rotation, wring the lead leg thigh like a wet towel, expressing a whirlpool rotation that spirals upward or downward. The Knee must not recede!

向前進攻帶動你的胳膊肘在你們手裡

• To attack forward drive your elbow into your hand.
(The humorous bone lever must initiate
and drive the forearm)

朝目標始終對準你的前臂

• Always align your forearm with/toward the target.

每牛年有兩個角，四個蹄子

• Every Ox has two horns, and four hooves.
- Martial interpretation -
*(Conseal within every single action no less than
three attacks, at Minimum double your
striking ratio to that of your attacker.)*
Stating a Ox has two horns, and four hooves expresses
that any one of those anatomical weapons can injure or
kill, all six guarantee death.

在水面上跳石有一條路由

• A skipping stone on water has one route.

- Martial interpretation -

(Be aware of adjacent and indirect targets that are along
a single route of attack. Ricochet from target to target
in single actions.)

清單彈道導彈旋轉補充力量和潛力，
顯示穩定的攻擊者的每一個動作

• Manifest ballistic rotation in every action for added
power and potential to dis-stabilize the attacker.

不聞不若聞之，聞之不若見之，見之不若
知之，知之不若行之；學至於行之而止矣
不闻不若闻之，闻之不若见之，见之不若
知之，知之不若行之；学至于行之而止矣

Literally: Not hearing is not as good as hearing, hearing is not as good as seeing, seeing is not as good as mentally knowing, mentally knowing is not as good as acting; true learning continues up to the point that action comes forth

Common: I hear and I forget; I see and I remember; I do and I understand. *Moral:* You can only understand something by trying it yourself. *Revised:* Tell me and I [will] forget. Show me and I [will] remember. Involve me and I [will] understand.

小洞不补，大洞吃苦

Translation: A small hole not mended in time will become a big hole much more difficult to mend. Meaning: This proverb tells us that if a trivial problem is not solved in time, it will become a serious one.

读书须用意，一字值千金

Translation: Intention of required study, the word worth a thousand gold.

Meaning: When reading, don't let a single word escape your attention; one word may be worth a thousand pieces of gold. This proverb stresses the fact that study requires undivided attention. And if there is something you don't understand, interrupt yourself. Only in this way can study be rewarded.

讀萬卷書不如行萬裡路,
读万卷书不如行万里路

Literally: Reading ten thousand books is not as useful
as traveling ten thousand miles.
Closest English equivalent:
An ounce of practice is worth more than a pound of
theory. *Meaning:* Practical experience is more
useful than theory.

風向轉變時,有人築牆,有人造風車, 风向转
变时,有人筑墙,有人造风车

Literally: When the wind of change blows, some build
walls, while others build windmills.
English equivalent: When one door closes, another
opens. *Meaning:* When your life seems to be changing, it is better to adapt to the changes
rather than be stubborn.

福無重至,禍不單行, 福无重至,祸不单行

Literally: Fortune does not come twice. Misfortune
does not come alone.
Meaning: The emphasis is on "misfortune doesn't
come alone". It's often used as an opener or
exclamation, when people talk about
coincidental events of misfortune.

害人之心不可有, 害人之心不可有

Literally: Do not harbour intentions to hurt others.
Do not desire to hurt others in the
depths of your heart.

良藥苦口, 良药苦口
— *Translation:* Good medicine tastes bitter.
— *Meaning:* We often don't heed good advice.
— *English equivalent:*
The Advice most needed is often the least heeded.

肉包子打狗, 肉包子打狗
— *Literally:*
To hit a dog with a meat-bun.
— *Interpretation:*
Punishment gives less incentive than a reward.
— *Other possible interpretation:*
There might be a radically different and much
more effective way to solve a problem.

死馬當活馬醫, 死马当活马医
— *Literally:* Try to save the dead horse
as if it is still alive.
— *English equivalent:* Nothing is impossible.
— *Meaning:* Do the impossible, for it may
truly be possible.

師傅領進門, 修行在個人, 师傅领进门,
修行在个人
— *Meaning:* Teachers open the door.
You enter by yourself.
— *English equivalent:* You can lead the horse
to the water, but you can't make it drink.

授人以魚不如授人以漁, 授人以
鱼不如授人以渔
— *Literally:* Teach a man to take a fish is not equal to teach a man how to fish.
English equivalent: Give a man a fish and you feed him for a day. Teach a man to fish and you feed him for a lifetime.

樹倒猢猻散, 树倒猢狲散
Literally: When the tree falls, the monkeys scatter.
English equivalent: Rats desert a sinking ship.
Usage: When a leader loses power, his followers become disorganized.

水能載舟, 亦能覆舟, 水能载舟, 亦能覆舟
Literally: Not only can water float a boat, it can sink it also. Moral: Nature can help and harm you. The people(water) can raise someone(boat) to power, but can also take it away(sink).
English equivalent: The knife cuts both ways.

三思而后行
Translation: Think three times before you move.
English equivalent: Measure thrice, cut once.
Meaning: One should always act only after due consideration. A hasty action may involve an improper consideration of important aspects.

一分耕耘, 一分收穫, 一分耕耘, 一分收获
Literally: If one does not plow, there will be no harvest. **English equivalent:** You reap what you sow; Honey is sweet, but the bees sting.

有錢能使鬼推磨, 有钱能使鬼推磨
If you have money you can make the
devil push your grind stone.
English equivalents:
Money talks; Money makes the world go round.
Meaning: Money is power.

自助者天助, 自助者天助
Literally: Those who help themselves, God will help.
Meaning: God will help those who help themselves.

After three days without reading,
talk becomes flavorless.

Be not afraid of growing slowly,
be afraid only of standing still.

A book is like a garden carried in the pocket.

A book holds a house of gold.

A closed mind is like a closed book;
just a block of paper.

A fall into a ditch makes you wiser.

If you do not study hard when young you'll
end up bewailing your failures as you grow up.

If a son is uneducated, his dad is to blame.

A Jade stone is useless before it is processed;
a man is good-for-nothing until he is educated.

The longer the night lasts,
the more our dreams will be.

Of all the stratagems, to know
when to quit is the best.

One cannot refuse to eat just because there
is a chance of being choked.

Never Add legs to the snake after you have
finished drawing it.

An ant may well destroy a whole dam.

Behind an able man there are
always other able men.

Butcher the donkey after it finished
his job on the mill.

A dish of carrot hastily cooked may still have
soil uncleaned off the vegetable.

Dismantle the bridge shortly after crossing it.

Distant water won't help to put out a
fire close at hand.

Distant water won't quench
your immediate thirst.

Do not employ handsome servants.

If you do not want others to know what you
have done? Better not have done it
in the first place.

Better a diamond with a flaw than
a pebble without one.

Better do a good deed near at home than go
far away to burn incense.

Better to light a candle than
to curse the darkness.

A camel standing amidst a flock of sheep.

A clear conscience never fears
a knocking at midnight.

A crane standing amidst a flock of chickens.

Crows everywhere are equally black.

A dog won't forsake his master because of his
poverty; a son never deserts his mother for her
homely appearance.

Dream different dreams while on the same bed.

If you want happiness for an hour; take a nap. If
you want happiness for a day; go fishing. If you
want happiness for a month; get married. If you
want happiness for a year; inherit a fortune.
If you want happiness for a lifetime; help
someone else.

To not believe in one's dreams is to spend all of
one's life asleep.

There is only one pretty child in the world and
every mother has it.

A good fortune may forbode a bad luck, which
may in turn disguise a good fortune.

Have a mouth as sharp as a dagger
but a heart as soft as tofu.

Have one's ears pierced only before
the wedding ceremony starts.

A horse cannot gain weight if not fed with extra fodder during the night; a man cannot become wealthy without earnings apart from his regula salaries.

How can you expect to find ivory in a dog's mouth?

If you have never done anything evil, you should not be worrying about devils to knock at your door.

An inch of time is an inch of gold but you can't buy that inch of time with an inch of gold.

Lift a stone only to drop on your own feet.

Once bitten by a snake, he/she is scared all his/her life at the mere sight of a rope.

No wind, no waves.

An overcrowded chicken farm produce fewer eggs.

Pick up a sesame seed but lose sight of a watermelon.

Play a harp before a cow.

Paper can't wrap up a fire.

Reshape one's foot to try to fit into a new shoe.

Regular feet can't be affected by irregular shoes.

Shed no tears until seeing the coffin.

A smile will gain you ten more years of life.

A sly rabbit will have three openings to its den.

Some prefer carrot while others like cabbage.

Three humble shoemakers brainstorming will
make a great statesman.

You can't catch a cub without going
into the tiger's den.

You think you lost your horse? Who knows, he
may bring a whole herd back to you someday.

You won't help shoots grow by
pulling them up higher.

You can't expect both ends of a
sugar cane are as sweet.

Your fingers can't be of the same length.

Age and time do not wait for people.

Attack is the best defense.

Bad things never walk alone.

There are always ears on the
other side of the wall.

A tiger never returns to his prey
he did not finish off.

Vicious as a tigeress can be,
she never eats her own cubs.

We are not so much concerned if you are slow
as when you come to a halt.

A weasel comes to say Happy
New Year to the chickens.

When you are poor, neighbors close by will
not come; once you become rich, you'll be
surprised by visits from (alleged) relatives afar.

Without rice, even the cleverest
housewife cannot cook.

Do not use a hatchet to remove a fly
from your friend's forehead.

With true friends...even water drunk
together is sweet enough.

To attract good fortune, spend a new coin on
an old friend, share an old pleasure with a new
friend, and lift up the heart of a true friend by
writing his name on the wings of a dragon.

Mankind fears an evil man
but heaven does not.

Not the cry, but the flight of the wild duck,
leads the flock to fly and follow.

Not wine...men intoxicate themselves; Not
vice...men entice themselves.

A dog won't forsake his master because of his poverty; a son never deserts his mother for her homely appearance.

Even a hare will bite when it is cornered.

Once on a tiger's back, it is hard to alight.

Mend the pen only after the sheep are all gone.

One monk shoulders water by himself; two can still share the labor among them. When it comes to three, they have to go thirsty.

Only when all contribute their firewood can they build up a strong fire.

One joy scatters a hundred griefs.

Flies never visit an egg that has no crack.

How can you put out a fire set on a cart-load of firewood with only a cup of water?

It is easy to dodge a spear that comes in front of you but hard to keep harms away from an arrow shot from behind.

Kill a chicken before a monkey.
Kill one to warn a hundred.

A bird does not sing because it has an answer.
It sings because it has a song.

A bit of fragrance clings to the hand that gives flowers.

A book holds a house of gold.

A book is like a garden carried in the pocket.

A book tightly shut is but a block of paper.

A child's life is like a piece of paper on
which every person leaves a mark.

A diamond with a flaw is worth more
than a pebble without imperfections.

A filthy mouth will not utter decent language.

A fool judges people by the presents they give him.

A gem is not polished without rubbing,
nor a man perfected without trials.

A nation's treasure is in its scholars.

A rat who gnaws at a cat's tail invites destruction.

Be not afraid of growing slowly,
be afraid only of standing still.

Be the first to the field and the last to the couch.

Deep doubts, deep wisdom;
small doubts, little wisdom.

Dig the well before you are thirsty.

Do good, reap good; do evil, reap evil.

Do not fear going forward slowly;
fear only to stand still.

Do not remove a fly from your friend's
forehead with a hatchet.

Don't open a shop unless you like to smile.

Each generation will reap what the
former generation has sown.

Give a man a fish and you feed him for a day.
Teach a man to fish and you feed him for a lifetime.

He who asks is a fool for five minutes,
but he who does not ask remains a fool forever.

He who is drowned is not troubled by the rain.

He who strikes the first blow admits
he's lost the argument.

If heaven made him, earth can
find some use for him.

If you are patient in one moment of anger,
you will escape a hundred days of sorrow.

If you bow at all, bow low.

If you don't want anyone to know, don't do it.

Keep your broken arm inside your sleeve.

Not until just before dawn do people sleep best;
not until people get old do they become wise.

Raise your sail one foot and you get ten feet of wind.

Teachers open the door. You enter by yourself.

The gem cannot be polished without friction,
nor man perfected without trials.

The miracle is not to fly in the air,
or to walk on the water;
but to walk on the earth.

The palest ink is better than the best memory.

To know the road ahead, ask those coming back.

When you drink the water, remember the spring.

When you have only two pennies left in the world,
buy a loaf of bread with one, and share
the other with a friend.

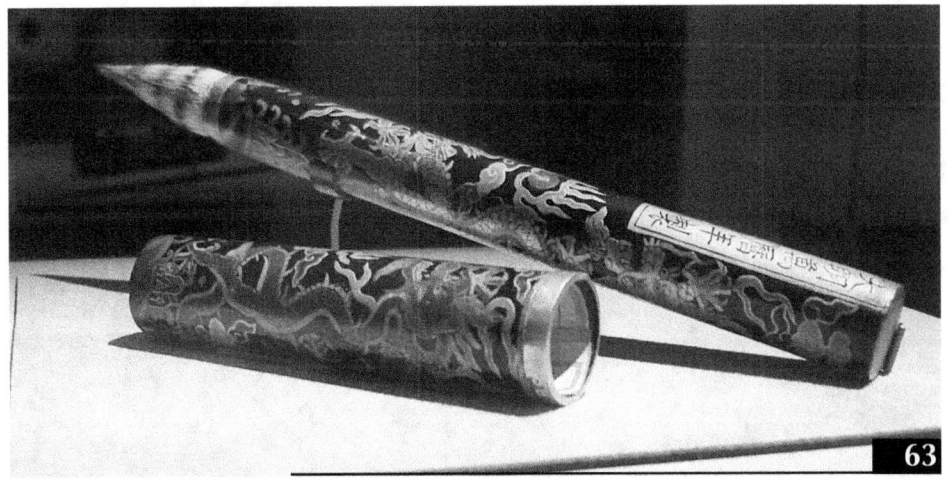

人心齐，泰山移
- When people work with one mind,
they can even remove Mount Taishan.

明人不用细说，响鼓不用重捶
- People of good sense or expertise need
only a hint to understand any matter.

花有重开日，人无再少年
- Flowers may bloom again, but a person
never has the chance to be young again.
So don't waste your time.

顾左右而言他
-Turning aside and changing the subject.

几家欢喜几家愁
- Some are happy, some have worries.
Or one man's disaster is another man's delight.

人无完人，金无足赤
- It is as impossible to find a perfect man as it is to find 100
percent pure gold.

有借有还，再借不难
- Timely return of a loan makes it easier to borrow a second time.

失败是成功之母
- Failure is mother of success.

人过留名，雁过留声
-A person leaves a reputation, bad or good, behind wherever he works or stays.

万事俱备，只欠东风
- Everything is ready except the east wind. This proverb instructs that everything is ready except what is crucial.

常将有日思无日，莫将无时想有时
- When rich, think of poverty, but don't think of riches when you are poor. This proverb indicates that frugality is the best policy: Be frugal even when you are rich, and don't dream of riches when you are poor, but work hard and be thrifty.

塞翁失马，焉知非福

-A bad thing may become a good thing under certain conditions. According to the book 'Huainanzi - Lessions of Human World' , an old man living in a border region lost his horse and people came to comfort him, but he said 'This may be a blessing in disguise, who knows?' Indeed, the horse later returned to the man and brought him a better horse.

学而不思则罔，思而不学则殆

- Learning without thought means labour lost; thought without learning is perilous.

书到用时方恨少

It is when you are using what you have learned from books that you wish you had read more. This proverb reminds us that we can never read widely enough.

千军易得，一将难求

It is easy to find a thousand soldiers, but hard to find a good general. This proverb notes the difficulty of finding an outstanding leader.

小洞不补，大洞吃苦

A small hole not mended in time
will become a big hole much more
difficult to mend. This proverb tells
us that if a trivial problem is not solved in time,
it will become a serious and knotty one.

读书须用意，一字值千金

When reading, don't let a single word
escape your attention; one word may
be worth a thousand pieces of gold.
This proverb stresses the fact that
study requires undivided attention.
No single word should be passed
over before we fully understand it.
Only in this way can study be rewarded.

有理走遍天下，无理寸步难行

With justice on your side, you can go anywhere;
without it, you can't take a step.
This proverb stresses the fact that
righteousness will see you through all difficulties,
whereas without it your progress will be
hampered from the very start.

麻雀虽小，五脏俱全

Small as it is, the sparrow has all the vital organs.

但愿人长久，千里共婵娟

Wish us a long life to share the beauty of
this graceful moonlight, even thousands
miles apart. -Sayings and everything we
can think of about Mid-Autumn Festival.

听君一席话，胜读十年书

Listen to your advice, better than reading books for ten years.

路遥知马力，日久见人心

As distance tests a horse's strength,
so does time reveal a person's real character.
This saying tells us that a long period of
testing is needed to understand
one's nature and capabilities.

灯不拨不亮，理不辩不明

An oil lamp becomes brighter after trimming,
a truth becomes clearer after being discussed.
This saying tells us that facing a complicated
problem, only by discussion and debate
can we get the correct answer. Truth
develops through the comparison of ideas.

凡人不可貌相，海水不可斗量

As a man cannot be known by his looks,
neither can the sea be fathomed by a gourd.
This proverb notes that judging by appearance
may lead to serious mistakes.

桂林山水甲天下

Guilin's mountain and water scenery
is the best under heaven.

三人一条心，黄土变成金

If people are of one heart, even the yellow
earth can become gold. This proverb tells
us that as long as people are unified,
any goal can be achieved.

当局者迷,旁观者清

The spectators see more of the game
than the players. This proverb points out that
a person involved in a matter usually does
not have a comprehensive overview of it
due to too much concentration on gains
and losses, while the onlookers, who have
a calmer and more objective attitude,
have a better grasp of what is going on.

大处着想，小处着手

Keep the general goal in sight while tackling
daily tasks. This proverb advises us to always
keep the overall situation in mind and be
far-sighted while we set our hands
to mundane business.

吃一堑，长一智

A fall into the pit, a gain in your wit.
This proverb's messages is: Having gone
through a setback, one will have gained
experience and wisdom, which will be
useful if only one can take warning and
learn something from the setback.

不能一口吃成胖子

Keep going with your Chinese, you just started.
Don't give up! You can't get fat on one just one mouthful.

风无常顺，兵无常胜

A boat can't always sail with the wind;
an army can't always win battles.
This proverb urges us to be fully prepared
for difficulties and setbacks: It is impossible
to have smooth sailing all the time.

水满则溢
Water surges only to overflow.
This proverb points out that: things
turn into their opposites when
they reach their extremes.

有缘千里来相会
Fate brings people together no matter
how far apart they may be. This proverb
points out that human relationships
are decreed by Fate.

哑巴吃饺子,心里有数
When a mute person eats dumplings (饺子 jiaozi),
he knows how many he has eaten,
even though he cannot speak.
We use this saying to point someone
knowing the situation quite well,
yet saying nothing.

只要功夫深，铁杵磨成针
If you work hard enough at it, you can
grind even an iron rod down to a needle.
This proverb encourages us to persevere in
whatever we undertake. Just as the
English proverb has it:
"Constant drilling can wear away a stone".

种瓜得瓜, 种豆得豆
As a man sows, so shall he reap.
This proverb warns that one receives
just returns for one's actions;
good for good, and evil for evil.

善有善报
Do well and have well.

人逢喜事精神爽
A merry heart makes a cheerful countenance.

水滴石穿, 绳锯木断
Dripping water pierces a stone; a saw
made of rope cuts through wood. Meaning:
Patience and persistence can berk through
anything,no matter how gerat the difficulty.

一日之计在于晨
A day's planning is done in the morning.

君子之交淡如水
The friendship of a gentleman is insipid as water.

月到中秋分外明, 每逢佳节倍思亲
The moon is the most bright on the
Mid-Autumn Festival, and the homesick
feeling will be stronger during this traditional festival .

读万卷书不如行万里路
It is better to travel ten thousand miles
than to read ten thousand books.

静以修身
Quiet thoughts mend the body.

强龙难压地头蛇
Even a dragon (from the outside) finds
it hard to control a snake in its old haunt.
This means: Powerful outsiders can
hardly afford to neglect local bullies.

一步一个脚印儿
Every step leaves its print; work
steadily and make solid progress.

一个萝卜一个坑儿
One radish, one hole. Each has his own
task, and nobody is dispensable.

宰相肚里好撑船/宽容大量
A prime minister's mind should be broad
enough for poling a boat.

冰冻三尺,非一日之寒
It takes more than one cold day for a
river to freeze three feet deep.

三个和尚没水喝
Three monks have no water to drink.
This means 'Too many cooks spoil the broth'.
ESL: The English idiom means there are
too many people trying to do something,
so they make a mess of it.

一人难称百人心/众口难调
It is hard to please everyone.

千里之行,始于足下
A thousand-li journey is started by taking the first step.

国以民为本,民以食为天
People as the root of the country, and
food is the first necessity of people.

没有规矩不成方圆
Nothing can be accomplished
without norms or standards.

前怕狼,后怕虎
Fear the wolf in front and the tiger
behind/ hesitate in doing something.

青出于蓝而胜于蓝
Indigo blue is obtained from the indigo
plant, but such color is bluer than the
plant itself; the disciple has surpassed the master.

老骥伏枥，志在千里
An old warhorse in the stable still
longs to gallop a thousnad li.
Meaning: One who still cherishes
high aspirations in spite of age.

十年树木,百年树人
It takes ten years to grow trees but
a hundred years to rear people.

李青蓮

李白字太白母夢長庚星因名
白生蜀之青蓮鄉賀知章見其文嘆曰
子謫仙人也言于帝詔供奉翰林帝
嘗坐沉香亭意有所感欲得白
為樂章時白已醉以水灑面稍
解立成清平調三篇太真笑領歌
意會白醉使高力士脫靴力士
素貴恥之摘其語以激太真
欲官白宮中
輒沮之白
遂散放日
沉飲弄月
采石江
而卒

兵不厌诈
Nothing is too deceitful in war.

木已成舟,生米煮成熟饭
The timber has been turned into a boat already.
The rice is already cooked. *Meaning:*
What's done cannot be undone.

身体力行
Practice what you preach.

惩前毖后
Learn from past mistakes to avoid future ones.

化干戈为玉帛
To bury the hatchets and work for peace.

严师出高徒
Good pupils are to be brought up by strict teachers.

哀兵必胜
An oppressed army fighting with
desperate courage is sure to win.

李青蓮

李白字太白母夢長庚星因名
白生蜀之青蓮鄉賀知章見其
文嘆曰子謫仙人也言于帝詔供
奉翰林帝嘗坐沉香亭意有
所感欲得白為樂章時白已醉
以水灑面稍解立成清平調三
篇太真笑領歌意會白醉使
高力士脫靴力士素貴恥之摘
其語以激太真帝欲官白宮中
輒沮之白迷教放日沉飲弄月
采石江而卒

留得青山在，不怕没材烧
Where there is life, there is hope.

祸从口出
Disaster emanates from a careless talk.

静以修身
A light heart lives long.

逆境出人才
Adversity makes a man wise, not rich.

事实胜于雄辩
Actions speak louder than words.

蜡烛照亮别人,却毁灭了自己
A candle lights others and consumes itself.

不会撑船怪河弯
A bad workman always blames his tools.

保持紀律進行自己的道德作為一個武術家
Sau Gay Loot Soong Syeung Moh Duck
Remain disciplined, conduct yourself ethically as a martial artist.

實踐禮貌和公義服務社會並尊重你的長輩
Ming Lai Yee Ngoy Goke Juen Chun
Practice courtesy and righteousness, serve the community
and respect your elders.

愛你的同學團結起來避免衝突
Ngoy Toang Hock Tuen Geet Loke Kwun
Love your fellow students, be united and avoid conflicts.

刻苦訓練保持自己的技能
Kun Leen Jop Gay But Lay Sun
Train diligently, maintain your skills.

學習如何開發精神安寧放棄從參數和打架
Hock Yeung Hay Gai Lum Dau Jung
Learn to develop spiritual tranquility, abstain
from arguments and fights.

參與社會保守你的舉止溫柔
Syeung Chue Sai Tai Doh Wun Mun
Participate in society, be conservative
and gentle in your manners.

幫助弱者很年輕老的用你的良好的人類門派技能
Foo Yeuk Siu Yee Moh Foo Yun
Help the weak and the very young and old, use your
martial skills for the good of humanity.

傳遞的傳統，保護這個中國藝術和其行為規則
Gai Gwong Soy Hoan Gay Joh Fun
Pass on the tradition, preserve this Chinese art
and its Rules of Conduct.

您必須是兇猛的衝突時
Gau Foong Yiu Han
You must be ferocious when clashing.

Thirty-Six Stratagems 三十六計

The Thirty-Six Stratagems are a Chinese essay used to illustrate a series of stratagems used in politics, war, as well as in civil interaction, often through unorthodox or deceptive means.

The Stratagems are often misnamed as strategies; however, a stratagem (synonymous with ruse) is not the same thing as a strategy (being a long-term plan or outline).

> Winning Stratagems (勝戰計)
> Enemy Dealing Stratagems (敵戰計)
> Attacking Stratagems (攻戰計)
> Chaos Stratagems (混戰計)
> Proximate Stratagems (並戰計)
> Desperate Stratagems (敗戰計)

Origin

The Thirty-Six Stratagems, The name of the collection comes from the Book of Qi, in its seventh biographical volume, Biography of Wáng Jìngzé (王敬則傳／王敬则传).[1] Wáng was a general who had served Southern Qi since the first Emperor Gao of the dynasty. When Emperor Ming came to power and executed many members of the court and royal family for fear that they would threaten his reign, Wáng believed that he would be targeted next and rebelled. As Wáng received news that Xiao Baojuan, son and crown prince of Emperor Ming, had escaped in haste after learning of the rebellion, he commented that "of the thirty-six stratagems of Lord Tán, retreat was his best, you father and son should run for sure."Lord Tán here refers to general Tan Daoji of the Liu Song Dynasty, who was forced to retreat after his failed attack on Northern Wei, and Wáng mentioned his name in contempt as an example of cowardice.

It should be noted that the number thirty-six was used by Wáng as a figure of speech in this context, and is meant to denote numerous stratagems instead of any specific number. Wáng's choice of this term was in reference to the I Ching, where six is the number of Yin that shared many characteristics with the dark schemes involved in military strategy. As thirty-six is the square of six, it therefore acted as a metaphor for numerous strategies. Since Wáng was not referring to any thirty-six specific stratagems however, the thirty-six proverbs and their connection to military strategies and tactics are likely to have been created after the fact, with the collection only borrowing its name from Wáng's saying.

The Thirty-Six Stratagems have variably been attributed to Sun Tzu from the Spring and Autumn Period of China, or Zhuge Liang of the Three Kingdoms period, but neither are regarded as the true author by historians. Instead, the prevailing view is that the Thirty-Six Stratagems may have originated in both written and oral history, with many different versions compiled by different authors throughout Chinese history. Some stratagems reference occurrences in the time of Sun Bin, approx. 150 years after Sun Wu's death.

The original hand-copied paperback that is the basis of the current version was believed to have been discovered in China's Shaanxi province, of an unknown date and author, and put into print by a local publisher in 1941. The Thirty-Six Stratagems only came to the public's attention after a review of it was published in the Chinese Communist Party's Guangming Daily (光明日報／光明日报)

The Thirty-Six Stratagems are divided into a preface, six chapters containing six stratagems each, and an afterword that was incomplete with missing text. The first three chapters generally describe tactics for use in advantageous situations, whereas the last three chapters contain stratagems that are more suitable for disadvantageous situations. They are in the form of four-character idioms. Each proverb is accompanied by a short comment, no longer than a sentence or two, that explains how said proverb is applicable to military tactics. These 36 Chinese proverbs are related to 36 battle scenarios in Chinese history and folklore, predominantly of the Warring States Period and the Three Kingdoms Period.

Winning Stratagems When In A Superior Position
勝戰計-

1. Deceive the heavens to cross the ocean, - or - Cross the sea under camouflage - 瞞天過海 -

This means to create a front that eventually becomes imbued with an atmosphere or impression of familiarity, within which the strategist may maneuver unseen while all eyes are trained to see obvious famil-iarities. Combat application: Hiding your motion in motion. Example; light hopping in sparring can hide your attack.

Prepare too much and you lose sight of the big picture; what you see often you do not doubt. Yin (the art of deception) is in Yang (acting in open). Too much Yang (transparency) hides Yin (true ruses). This stratagem references an episode in 643 AD, when Emperor Taizong of Tang, balked from crossing the sea to a campaign against Koguryo. His general Xue Rengui thought of a stratagem to get the emperor across and allay his fear of seasickness: on a clear day, the emperor was invited to meet a wise man. They entered through a dark tunnel into a hall where they feasted. After feasting several days, the Emper-or heard the sound of waves and realised that he had been lured onto a ship! General Xue drew aside the curtains to reveal the ocean and confessed that they had already crossed the sea: Upon discovering this, the emperor decided to carry on and later completed the suc-cessful campaign.

This stratagem means that you can mask your real goals, by using the ruse of a fake goal that everyone takes for granted, until the real goal is achieved. Tactically, this is known as an 'open feint'; in front of ev-eryone, you point west, when your goal is actually in the east. By the time everyone realised it, you have already achieved your goal. Harro von Senger notes in the German-Language "Die List" that to grasp the full meaning, it would be something like "to deceive the holy virgin Mary" in the West.

This stratagem makes use of the human failing to become unaware of common everyday activities, or events that appear normal. The best secrets are carried out in broad daylight. The best hoax is to repeat it so often that people are convinced that the next move is also a hoax. When this happens, it is the best moment to carry out one's previously hidden true objective.

2. Surround one state to save another.
圍魏救趙- Besiege Wei to rescue Zhao

When a strong group is about to take over a weaker group, a third part can "have its cake and eat it too," gaining a good reputation by attacking the aggressor in apparent behalf of the defender, and also eventually absorb the weakened defender to boot, without incurring the same opprobrium that would be leveled at outright aggression. Combat application: Protecting a loved one or friend.

When the enemy is too strong to be attacked directly, then attack something he holds dear. Know that he cannot be superior in all things. Somewhere there is a gap in the armour, a weakness that can be attacked instead.

The origin of this proverb is from the Warring States Period. The state of Wèi attacked Zhao and laid siege to its capital Handan. Zhào turned to Qí for help, but the Qí general Sun Bin determined it would be unwise to meet the army of Wèi head on, so he instead attacked their capital at Daliang. The army of Wèi retreated in haste, and the tired troops were ambushed and defeated at the Battle of Guiling, with the Wèi general Pang Juan fled on the field. Note that this campaign is also described explicitly in the Art of War of Master Sun Bin the younger.

The idea here is to avoid a head on battle with a strong enemy, and instead strike at his weakness elsewhere. This will force the strong enemy to retreat in order to support his weakness. Battling against the now tired and low-morale enemy will give a much higher chance of success.

3. Borrow a sword to attack another.
借刀殺人- Kill with a borrowed knife
(kill someone through the agency of another)

When one side in a conflict is weakening, it may draw its own friends into battle, thus delivering a blow to its enemy while conserving its own strength. Combat application: Defeat the enemy through the use of their own power or that of another, also Literally disarm the attacker and use their weapon.

Attack using the strength of another (in a situation where using one's own strength is not favourable). Trick an ally into attacking him, bribe an official to turn traitor, or use the enemy's own strength against him. The idea here is to cause damage to the enemy by getting a 3rd party to do the deed.

4. Face the weary in a condition of ease.
以逸待勞 -Wait at ease for the fatigued enemy or Leisurely await the laboured.

You force others to expend energy while you preserve yours. You tire opponents out by sending them on wild goose chases, or by making them come to you from far away while you stand your ground. Combat application: Stay out of your attackers range and make them expend energy on useless attacks.
It is an advantage to choose the time and place for battle. In this way you know when and where the battle will take place, while your enemy does not. Encourage your enemy to expend his energy in futile quests while you conserve your strength. When he is exhausted and confused, you attack with energy and purpose.

The idea is to have your troops well-prepared for battle, in the same time that the enemy is rushing to fight against you. This will give your troops a huge advantage in the upcoming battle, of which you will get to select the time and place.

5. Plunge into a fire to pull off a robbery.
趁火打劫 - Loot a burning house.

You use others'troubles as opportunities to gain something for yourself. Combat application: Take advantage of your attackers misfortune, for example if the sun, rain, wind gets in their eyes, of they become distracted etc. When a country is beset by internal conflicts, when disease and famine ravage the population, when corruption and crime are rampant, then it will be unable to deal with an outside threat. This is the time to attack.

Keep gathering internal information about an enemy. If the enemy is currently in its weakest state ever, attack it without mercy and totally destroy it to prevent future troubles.

6. Feint east, strike west. 聲東擊西
- Make faint to the east but attack in the west

You spread misleading information about your intentions, or make false suggestions, in order to induce the opponent to concentrate his defenses on one front and thereby leave another front vulnerable to attack.

Combat application: Feint, fake. In sparring fake a low kick and follow with a high strike when your attacker lowers their defense. In any battle the element of surprise can provide an overwhelming advantage. Even when face to face with an enemy, surprise can still be employed by attacking where he least expects it. To do this you must create an expectation in the enemy's mind through the use of a feint. The idea here is to get the enemy to focus his forces in a location, and then attack elsewhere which would be weakly defended.

Enemy Dealing Stratagems (敵戰計)

7. Make something from nothing.
無中生有 - Produce something out of nothing
Create something from nothing (無中生有／无中生有)

You create a false idea in the mind of the opponent, and fix it in his mind as a reality. In particular, this means that you convey the impression that you have what you do not, to the end that you may appear formidable and thus actually obtain a security that you had not enjoyed before.

Combat application: I once used my wallet as a pretend cell phone to scare off a car full of car thieves. From a distance they thought I was calling the police. This is similar to sticking your finger through your jacket and faking you have a gun. You could also pretend to know a stranger crossing the street, waving to them to plant the false idea in the attackers mind that you know them. A plain lie. Make somebody believe there was something when there is in fact nothing. One method of using this stratagem is to create an illusion of something's existence, while it does not exist. Another method is to create an illusion that something does not exist, while it does.

8. Cross the pass in the dark.
暗渡陳倉 - Advance to Chencang by a hidden path
Openly repair the gallery roads, but sneak through the passage of Chencang (明修棧道,暗渡陳倉／明修栈道, 暗渡陈仓)

You set up a false front, then penetrate the opponent's territory on other fronts while they are distracted by your false front. (pretend to prepare along one path while secretly going along another)

Combat application: Zig then Zag, fake left go right etc.

Deceive the enemy with an obvious approach that will take a very long time, while surprising him by taking a shortcut and sneak up

to him. As the enemy concentrates on the decoy, he will miss you sneaking up to him.

The phrase originated from the Chu-Han contention, where Liu Bang retreated to the lands of Sichuan to prepare for a confrontation with Xiang Yu. Once he was fully prepared, Liu Bang sent men to openly repair the gallery roads he had destroyed earlier, while secretly moving his troops towards Guanzhong through the small town of Chencang instead. When Xiang Yu received news of Liu Bang repairing the gallery roads, he dismissed the threat since he knew the repairs would take years to complete. This allowed Liu Bang to retake Guanzhong by surprise, and eventually led to his victory over Xiang Yu and the birth of the Han Dynasty.

This tactic is an extension of the "Make a sound in the east, then strike in the west" tactic. But instead of simply spreading misinformation to draw the enemy's attention, physical baits are used to increase the enemy's certainty on the misinformation. These baits must be easily seen by the enemy, to ensure that they draw the enemy's attention. At the same time, the baits must act as if what they meant to do what they were falsely doing, to avoid drawing the enemy's suspicion.

9. Watch the fire from the opposite bank of the river.
隔岸觀火 Watch the fire from the other side of the river (showing non-concernedness)
Watch the fires burning across the river.
(隔岸觀火／隔岸观火)

You calmly look on when adversaries experience internal troubles, waiting for them to destroy themselves.
Combat application: Take advantage of any environmental distractions or misfortunes your attacker may suffer. Crossing the street when faced with multiple attackers for example can disorganize the group if there is traffic. Delay entering the field of battle until all the other players have become exhausted fighting amongst themselves. Then go in at full strength and pick up the pieces.

10. Hide a sword in a smile.
笑裡藏刀 Conceal a knife in your smile
Hide a knife behind a smile (笑裏藏刀／笑里藏刀)

You ingratiate yourself with enemies, inducing them to trust you.
When you have their confidence, you can move against them in secret. Combat application: Don't let on you are about to attack.
Charm and ingratiate yourself to your enemy. When you have gained
his trust, move against him in secret.

11. One tree falls for another.
李代桃僵 - The plum dies for the apricot
Sacrifice the plum tree to preserve the peach tree
(李代桃僵)

Individual sacrifices may have to made to achieve a greater goal.
(substitute this for that) Combat application: Create a false opening
to bait the attacker into a trap. There are circumstances in which you
must sacrifice short-term objectives in order to gain the long-term
goal. This is the scapegoat stratagem whereby someone else suffers
the consequences so that the rest do not.

12. Take the sheep in hand as you go along.
Make off with a sheep in passing by. 順手牽羊
Take the opportunity to pilfer a goat.
(順手牽羊／顺手牵羊)

You take advantage of any opportunity, however small, and avail
yourself of any profit, however slight. This comes from the story of
a destitute traveler walking on a road. As he went along, he came
across a flock of sheep; making his way through them, when he
emerged from their midst he had a sheep with him. He behaved so
calmly and naturally, as it he had been leading his own sheep to

market all along, that the shepherd never noticed him. (Lead away a sheep in passing)

Combat application: Hide your attack in a natural unthreatening motions. While carrying out your plans be flexible enough to take advantage of any opportunity that presents itself, however small, and avail yourself of any profit, however slight.

Attacking Stratagems (攻戰計)

13. Beat the grass to startle the snakes.

打草驚蛇 - Beat the grass and frighten away the snake, Stomp the grass to scare the snake

(打草驚蛇／打草惊蛇)

When opponents are reserved and unfathomable, you create some sort of stir to see how they will react. Yagyfi mentions this, and also notes that it is used in Sun (Zen). Certain Sun sayings and stories are used primarily to test people and find out what they are like.

Combat application: Test your opponents reactions with hand strikes, low kicks, verbal attacks etc. Push their buttons. Do something un-aimed, but spectacular ("hitting the grass") to provoke a response of the enemy ("startle the snake"), thereby giving away his plans or position, or just taunt him. Do something unusual, strange, and unexpect-ed as this will arouse the enemy's suspicion and disrupt his thinking. More widely used as "[Do not] startle the snake by hitting the grass". An imprudent act will give your position or intentions away to the enemy.

14. Borrow a corpse to bring back a spirit.

借屍還魂 - Resurrect in a new guise, Borrow a corpse to resurrect the soul.

(借屍還魂／借尸还魂)

You don't use what everyone else is using, but use what others aren't using. This can mean reviving something that has dropped out of use through neglect, or finding uses for things that had hitherto been ignored or considered useless. (Raise the dead)

Combat application: Improvise a weapon from a natural object. Take an institution, a technology, a method, or even an ideology that has been forgotten or discarded and appropriate it for your own purpose. Revive something from the past by giving it a new purpose or bring to life old ideas, customs, or traditions and reinterpret them to fit your purposes.

15. Train a tiger to leave the mountains.
調虎離山 - Lure the tiger out of the mountain
Entice the tiger to leave its mountain lair
(調虎離山／调虎离山)

You don't go into the fastness of powerful opponents' territory, but induce them to come out of their stronghold.
Combat application: Bait your attacker with a false opening.
Never directly attack an opponent whose advantage is derived from its position. Instead lure him away from his position thus separating him from his source of strength.

16. Let the enemy leave in order to catch him
欲擒故縱 - Let the enemy off so to snare them
In order to capture, one must let loose
(欲擒故縱／欲擒故纵)

When you want to take captives, leave them on the loose for a while. (Let the enemy off so to snare them) Fleeing enemies may turn again and strike desperately if pursued too hotly. If they are given room to run, on the other hand, they scatter and lose their energy. Then they can be taken captive without further violence.

Combat application: Control your attackers motion, cutting off his options and force them where you want them to be, for example drawing an attacker in between two parked cars, a stair case etc.

Cornered prey will often mount a final desperate attack. To prevent this you let the enemy believe he still has a chance for freedom. His will to fight is thus dampened by his desire to escape. When in the end the freedom is proven a falsehood the enemy's morale will be defeated and he will surrender without a fight.

17. Toss out a glazed tile to draw a jade.
抛磚引玉 - Cast a brick to attract a gem
Tossing out a brick to get a jade gem
(抛磚引玉／抛砖引玉)

You present something of superficial or apparent worth to induce another party to produce something of real worth.
Combat application: Bait your attacker with a pretend opening.
Bait someone by making him believe he gains something or just make him react to it ("toss out a brick") and obtain something valuable from him in return ("get a jade gem").

This proverb is based on a story involving two famous poets of the Tang Dynasty. There was a great poet named Zhao Gu (趙嘏) and another lesser poet by the name of Chang Jian (常建). While Chang Jian was travelling in Suzhou, he heard news that Zhao Gu would be visiting a temple in the area.

Chang Jian wished to learn from the master poet, so he devised a plan and went to the temple in advance, then wrote a poem on the temple walls with only two of the four lines completed, hoping Zhao Gu would see it and finish the poem. Zhao Gu acted as Chang Jian foresaw, and from this story came the proverb.

18. To capture the brigands (rebels), capture their king.
擒賊先擒王 - (To kill a snake cut off the head)
Catch the ringleader first in order to capture all his bandit followers. or Defeat the enemy by capturing their chief (擒賊擒王／擒贼擒王)

When confronted with a massive opposition, you take aim at its central leadership. Combat application: Take out the leader or the most feared of the group and the group will usually become disorganized.If the enemy's army is strong but is allied to the commander only by money, superstition or threats, then take aim at the leader. If the commander falls the rest of the army will disperse or come over to your side. If, however, they are allied to the leader through loyalty then beware, the army can continue to fight on after his death out of vengeance.

Chaos Stratagems (混戰計)

19. Take the firewood out from under the pot.
釜底抽薪 - Take away the firewood under the cauldron, or Remove the firewood from under the pot (釜底抽薪)

When you cannot handle an adversary in a head-on confrontation, you can still win by undermining the enemy's resources and morale. (take drastic measures to strike at source of a problem)

Combat application: Again using the environment, for example tipping over furniture, drawing them onto higher ground (you're higher) etc. The idea being if you are of equal or inferior skills you must use strategy to succeed. If something must be destroyed, destroy the source.

20. Stir up the waters to catch fish.
渾水摸魚 - Fish in troubled water
Disturb the water and catch a fish
(渾水摸魚／浑水摸鱼)

You use confusion to your advantage, to take what you want. It may specifically mean taking advantage of a general or particular loss of direction in order to gather followers from among the uncommitted or disenfranchised. (try to take advantage of a disturbed situation to take in profits)

Combat application: Fighting with the sun to your back so it's in their eyes, or the wind. Bumping a car to activate the alarm to create confusion. Take advantage of your opponents distractions. Create confusion and use this confusion to further your own goals.

21. The gold cicada molts its shell.
金蟬脫殼 - Cast off the molted skin/gold cicada casts off its shell, or Slough off the cicada's golden shell (金蟬脫殼／金蝉脱壳)

This means leaving behind false appearances created for strategic purposes. Like the cicada shell, the facade remains intact, but the real action is now elsewhere. (escape unnoticed)

Combat application: Raise a hand high and kick low, toss something at your attackers face etc. It's a stratagem mainly used to escape from an enemy of superior force. Mask yourself. Either leave flamboyant traits behind, thus going incognito, or just masquerade yourself and create an illusion to fit your goals and distract others.

22. Lock the gates to catch the bandits.
關門捉賊 - Close the gate to catch the thieves
Shut the door to catch the thief (關門捉賊／关门捉贼)

You catch invading predators by not letting them get away. You don't let them get back to their homelands with what they can get from you. If they escape, you don't chase them, because you will thereby fall prey to the enemy's plot to wear you down. (Bolt the door to catch the thief)
Combat application: Stepping on your attackers foot, trapping their hands etc. To deliver capture the enemy, you must plan prudently if

you want to succeed. Do not rush into action. Before you "move in for the kill", first cut off your enemy's escape routes, and cut off any routes through which outside help can reach them.

23. Make allies at a distance, attack nearby. Korean: Weon gyo geon gong

遠交近攻 Befriend distant countries while attacking those nearby, Befriend a distant state while attacking a neighbour (遠交近攻／远交近攻)

When you are more vulnerable to those close by than you are to those far away, you can defend yourself by keeping those around you off balance, in the meantime cutting of their field of maneuver by securing a broader ring of alliances surrounding them.

Combat application: Concentrate on the immediate threat. It is known that nations that border each other become enemies while nations separated by distance and obstacles make better allies. When you are the strongest in one field, your greatest threat is from the second strongest in your field, not the strongest from another field. This policy is associated with Fan Sui of Qin, circa 269 BC.

24. Borrow the right of way to attack the neighbor.

假途伐虢 Conquer Hao after obtaining permittance to cross another country, or Obtain safe passage to conquer the State of Guo (假道伐虢)

You secure the temporary use of another party's facilities in order to move against a mutual enemy. After having used these facilities to prevail over the enemy, you then turn and use them against the party from whom you borrowed them. (forge neutral alliances)

Combat application: Use one attacker against the other. Move when fighting so they constantly cross each other and get in one another's way. Use an attackers weapon against the other attacker. Borrow the resources of an ally to attack a common enemy. Once the enemy is defeated, use those resources to turn on the ally that lent you them in

the first place. See Duke Xian of Jin.

Proximate Stratagems (並戰計)

25. Steal a beam to replace a pillar.
偷樑換柱 - Replace the beams and pillars with rotten timber, or Replace the beams with rotten timbers (偷梁換柱／偷梁換柱)

You try to recruit top talent from among allies, inducing them to join your concern. Combat application: Use negotiations and undermine their confidence, I remember one time an older master relates a time when a young punk with his friends started to harass him. He said to the harasser 'You know if you beat me up, all you did was beat up an old man. But on the other hand if I get a lucky shot in on you your friends will never let you forget an old man beat you. Either way it's not good' the young punk postured a little bit and then walked away. Attack the legs.

Disrupt the enemy's formations, interfere with their methods of operations, change the rules in which they are used to following, go contrary to their standard training. In this way you remove the supporting pillar, the common link that makes a group of men an effective fighting force.

26. Point at one to scold another.
指桑罵槐 - Point at the mulberry only to curse the locust. or - Point at the mulberry tree while cursing the locust tree (指桑罵槐／指桑骂槐)

You criticize indirectly, getting your point across without confrontation. (scold one person through another)
Combat application: If with another you can pretend it's their fault and you will take care of them. (of course this as to be explained wink, wink to your friend). To discipline, control, or warn others whose status or position excludes them from direct confrontation;

use analogy and innuendo. When names are not used directly, those accused cannot retaliate without revealing their complicity.

27. Feign ignorance without going crazy.
假癡不癲 - Feign foolishness, Feign madness but keep your balance (假痴不癲／假痴不癫)

You pretend to be stupid and ignorant, but avoid talking loosely. (Pretend madness without loosing the balance)
Combat application: Fake injury, sickness, stupidity etc. Hide behind the mask of a fool, a drunk, or a madman to create confusion about your intentions and motivations. Lure your opponent into underestimating your ability until, overconfident, he drops his guard. Then you may attack.

28. Let them climb the roof, then take away the ladder.
上屋抽梯 - Take away the ladder when the enemy is in the second floor. Remove the ladder when the enemy has ascended to the roof (上屋抽梯)

(Remove the ladder after the ascent) You maneuver enemies into a point of no return by baiting them with what look like advantages and opportunities. Combat application: Like Bruce Lee's character in the movie Enter the Dragon when he asked his challenger to take the small rowboat to the small island to fight. When the challenger got on the boat he set it adrift. A modern application would be to let them through the door first and then lock it behind them. With baits and deceptions, lure your enemy into treacherous terrain. Then cut off his lines of communication and avenue of escape. To save himself, he must fight both your own forces and the elements of nature.

29. Make flowers bloom on a tree.
樹上開花 - False flowers on a tree; Deck the tree with false blossoms (樹上開花／树上开花)

You dazzle and deceive the eyes of opponents by showy displays. (use decoys) Combat application: Fake and feint or shatter their

confidence with a demonstration of skill. I remember an older master discouraging a gang once by picking up a cobblestone from the street and breaking it in half. Tying silk blossoms on a dead tree gives the illusion that the tree is healthy. Through the use of artifice and disguise, make something of no value appear valuable; of no threat appear dangerous; of no use appear useful. This stratagem is identical to that of the Potemkin village.

30. Turn the guest into the host. 反客為主 - Make the guest the host, or Make the host and the guest exchange roles (反客為主／反客为主)

This is when a business is taken over by one of its own clients or consultants. Combat application: Use your attackers energy against them, when pushed-pull, when pulled-push.
Usurp leadership in a situation where you are normally subordinate. Infiltrate your target. Initially, pretend to be a guest to be accepted, but develop from inside and become the owner later.

Desperate Stratagems (敗戰計)

31 Scheme with beauties (Beauty Trap) 美人計 - Scheme with beauties, or The beauty trap (honey trap) (美人計／美人计)

This refers to using the charms of women to influence key figures in an adversary organization. The stratagem of (making use of) a beautiful woman (as decoy) Combat application: Use something attractive to the attacker, an opening, money, reward etc. A modern application could be dropping your wallet 'accidentally' as their eyes follow it attack.
Send your enemy beautiful women to cause discord within his camp. This stratagem can work on three levels.

First, the ruler becomes so enamoured with the beauty that he neglects his duties and allows his vigilance to wane. Second, other

males at court will begin to display aggressive behaviour that inflames minor differences hindering co-operation and destroying morale. Third, other females at court, motivated by jealousy and envy, begin to plot intrigues further exacerbating the situation.

32 Scheme with an empty castle (Empty castle ploy)
空城計 The stratagem of (open gates and) an emptied city (with soldiers waiting in ambush)
The empty fort strategy (空城計／空城计)

You appear weaker than you really are, so that opponents may defeat themselves by one of three reactions to your supposed weakness: they may become conceited and complacent, leading to their downfall; they may become arrogant and aggressive, leading to their destruction; or they may assume you are setting up an ambush, leading them to flee of their own accord.

Combat application: When weak appear strong, when strong appear weak. Don't let the attacker know your state, lure him by pretending to be weak, discourage him by appearing strong.

When the enemy is superior in numbers and your situation is such that you expect to be overrun at any moment, then drop all pretense of military preparedness and act calmly so that the enemy will think you are setting an ambush. This stratagem has to be used sparingly and only after one has first developed a reputation for military prowess. This also depends on having a clever opponent who, in perceiving a trap, may over-think his reaction.

33. Scheme with double agents.
(Sow discord in the enemy's camp)
反間計 The stratagem of sowing the seeds of discord (among the enemies) - Let the enemy's own spy sow discord in the enemy camp (反間計／反间计)

You compromise insiders of other organizations to get them to work for you. Combat application: In a multiple attack situation, attack in a fast, aggressive and unpredictable manner, to confuse the group. Undermine your enemy's ability to fight by secretly causing discord between him and his friends, allies, advisors, family, commanders, soldiers, and population. While he is preoccupied settling internal disputes, his ability to attack or defend, is compromised.

34. Scheme with self-inflicted wounds.
苦肉計 The stratagem of self-mutilation (in order to lure out the enemy) - Inflict injury on oneself to win the enemy's trust (苦肉計／苦肉计)

(Inflict minor injury on oneself to gain the enemy's trust) This a technique particularly for undercover agents: you make yourself look like a victim of your own people, in order to win the sympathy and confidence of enemies.

Combat application: Pretend to be injured or sick then attack. Pretending to be injured has two possible applications. In the first, the enemy is lulled into relaxing his guard since he no longer considers you to be an immediate threat. The second is a way of ingratiating yourself to your enemy by pretending the injury was caused by a mutual enemy.

35. Scheme in continuous circles (Interlocking stratagems) 連環計
The stratagem of combining rings (of various stratagems) - Chain stratagems (連環計／连环计)

When facing a more powerful enemy, you don't oppose by force, and don't concentrate all your resources on only one avenue of strategy; you keep different plans operating simultaneously in an overall scheme.

Combat application: Keep your awareness active, use what becomes available to you. Tip over furniture, throw objects etc.

In important matters, one should use several stratagems applied simultaneously after another as in a chain of stratagems. Keep different plans operating in an overall scheme; however, in this manner if any one stratagem fails, then the chain breaks and the whole scheme fails.

36. Know when It is best to run
(When retreat is the best option)
走為上計 The best stratagem is to run away
If all else fails, retreat (走為上／走为上)

When overwhelmed, you don't fight; you surrender, compromise, or flee. Surrender is complete defeat, compromise is half defeat, flight is not defeat. As long as you are not defeated, you have another chance to win. Combat application: Run!

If it becomes obvious that your current course of action will lead to defeat, then retreat and regroup. When your side is losing, there are only three choices remaining: surrender, compromise, or escape. Surrender is complete defeat, compromise is half defeat, but escape is not defeat. As long as you are not defeated, you still have a chance.

Gratitude and Special Thanks to...

Sifu Aaron Cantrell — Everything wing chun.com
Andrew Vachss — Author
Nancy R. Baker — Editor & technical consultant
Sensei Dale Wagner — Judo & Uechi Ryu
Guru Larry W. Gibson — Silat & Xingyiquan
Sifu Edmund Kwai — Wing Chun & South Mantis
Madame Tom Hoi Leong — Xingyiquan
Sifu R.L. Harris — Wing Chun & Xingyiquan
Sifu Elaine Emery — Tai Chi Chuan
Sifu Steve Cottrell — Wing Chun & Seven Star Mantis
Grand Master Brendan Lai — Seven Star Mantis
Sifu Lee Bing Choi — Wing Chun, South Mantis, Bak mei
Sensei Clyde Kimura — Judo & Jook Wan
Guru Carl Canliss — Balintawak, Kali Arnis
Sensei Jeff & Ann League — Aikiki Aikido
Sifu Steve Thompson — South Mantis & Bak Mei
Guru Steve Black — Kali & Silat,
Guru Steve Todd — Kali & Silat

Sifu Edward Robinson III — Taixuquan Six Elbows Kung Fu
Sifu Mike Reyes — Taixuquan Six Elbows Kung Fu
Sensei Russ Smith — Goju Ryu & Southern crane
Sifu Alex Do — Jook Lum Mantis & Bak mei
Sifu & Author Mark Wiley — Ngo cho kuen, Filipino Arts
Sifu Tyson Durr — Bak mei, Iron palm, Wing Chun
Sifu Rod Morgan — Iron palm, Wing Chun, Lung Ying Kuen
Guru Carl Magnuson — Kali, Baguazhang, Chen Tai Chi

• **Sifu Simon Lui**
— Lam Hung Pak Mei Athletic Association of Minnesota
Simon Lui Kung Fu Physical Institute
www.pakmeiassociation.com
E-Mail : pakmeiassociation@gmail.com